Josinaldo Roberto Rocha Gomes
Leiva C. Oliveira

Creation of a regulator for CPU power management

Josinaldo Roberto Rocha Gomes
Leiva C. Oliveira

Creation of a regulator for CPU power management

Development of a new CPU frequency regulator based on a study of the CPUFreq management module

ScienciaScripts

Imprint

Cover image: www.ingimage.com

This book is a translation from the original published under ISBN 978-613-9-66484-9.

Publisher:
Sciencia Scripts
is a trademark of
Dodo Books Indian Ocean Ltd. and OmniScriptum S.R.L publishing group

120 High Road, East Finchley, London, N2 9ED, United Kingdom
Str. Armeneasca 28/1, office 1, Chisinau MD-2012, Republic of Moldova, Europe
Printed at: see last page
ISBN: 978-620-8-03346-0

I dedicate this work to my family: **Josimar Gomes,** my father; **Nadja Rocha,** my mother; **Karla Oliveira,** my wife, and **Dolôres Neta,** my stepdaughter, for being admirable people in my existence and for pushing me to seek new life every day, depriving themselves of my company when I needed to dedicate myself to studying and giving me the opportunity to realise the dream of personal and professional growth. Also for their understanding and support in completing this work.

Blessed is the man who finds wisdom, and the man who acquires knowledge;
Because your merchandise is better than silverware, and your profit is greater than the finest gold.

Proverbs 3:13,14

ACKNOWLEDGEMENTS

To **God,** for giving me the opportunity to direct my life along the path of knowledge, wisdom and instruction. Also for giving me the knowledge to make the right choices that have brought me this far.

To my father, **Josimar Gomes,** who has always been fundamental to my growth, for his love and care for me, even with my limitations. I love him very much. Without his dedication I wouldn't have got this far.

To my mum, **Nadja Rocha,** who took care of me like no one else and always fought to give me a better and successful future. And she has fulfilled her role as a mother in my life extremely well. I love her very much too.

To my wife, **Karla Oliveira,** who has always supported me and fought with me so that I could get through this phase of my life. Having you by my side only gives me more strength and satisfaction in pursuing a career that is first and foremost about always being better.

To my supervisor, Professor **Leiva Casemiro,** for his invaluable guidance and contributions during the TCC I and TCC II courses, which culminated in the completion of this work.

To Professors **Daniel Sabino** and **Francisco de Assis,** for their careful reading of my Course Conclusion Paper I and for their valuable contributions to the product I am now presenting.

To my **teachers** on the Bachelor of Information Systems course at UFERSA/Campus

Angicos, from whom I was able to learn a little more and enrich my experiences. I would like to thank them for the wisdom and knowledge they have passed on to make me a competent professional.

To all the **friends** who have contributed directly or indirectly to my journey so far.

the opportunity to share work experiences in the New Talents and ICT in Education projects, in the context of Digital Inclusion.

To Professors **Araken de Medeiros** and **Daniel Sabino,** for the opportunity to carry out Scientific Initiation activities, as it was an essential experience in my academic training, leading me towards research and the world of science as an active subject.

To the Federal Rural University of the **Semi-Arid Region,** through the **Coordination of Community Affairs,** which, through the actions of academic permanence, provided me with basic financial conditions for part of my stay in Angicos/RN.

To my colleagues at the UFERSA/Angicos **Central Student Directory (DCE**), for the opportunity to constantly exercise their citizenship.

To the **city of Angicos,** for welcoming me and for the time I spent there, materialising my dream of studying at university and preparing me for a professional career.

Thank you!

SUMMARY

CHAPTER 1	**7**
CHAPTER 2	**10**
CHAPTER 3	**11**
CHAPTER 4	**20**
CHAPTER 5	**27**
CHAPTER 6	**34**
CHAPTER 7	**36**

SUMMARY

This work, entitled Study and development of a regulator for the energy management of a central processing unit, is based on a study of the regulators of the Kemel Linux module, CPUFreq, which manage the energy expenditure of the CPU(s). It aims to propose the construction of a new regulator for managing the energy expended by the processor. To this end, the work of LUIZ (2012) was important for its theoretical contributions. The aspects that most influence efficient energy saving in processors were investigated. The sampling rate, the utilisation calculation and the penalty calculation were the three indicators that made it feasible to process the information collected and used in the execution of our regulator, and consequently, to make satisfactory decisions on CPU power management. Based on the three indicators mentioned, a comparison was made between our regulator and the Onde- mand regulator, the latter being the standard regulator in the Linux Kernel from version 2.9 onwards. In terms of energy saving, our regulator was more efficient than Ondemand's, given that our regulator remained constant when changing the operating frequency of the CPU(s), both when increasing and decreasing these values. Ondemand, on the other hand, was just as efficient as our regulator when it came to increasing the frequency values, but when it came to decreasing them, it took longer to reduce the frequency, consequently using more energy than our regulator.

Keywords: Power management; CPUFreq; Linux kernel.

CHAPTER 1

INTRODUCTION

The energy efficiency of the Central Processing Unit (CPU or processor) in different types of computer systems - mobile devices, embedded computers, desktops, servers and clusters - plays an important role in the time and manner of execution of the workload to be processed by the CPU, as well as in the total energy consumption of the computer system.

For mobile devices and embedded computers powered by batteries, the energy efficiency of the CPU becomes a determining characteristic in the duration of the charge and, consequently, the time the user can use the device.

The quest to reduce energy consumption is a very important factor in maintaining and saving existing natural resources that are used in the manufacture and use of information and communications technologies (ICTs). After the main processor manufacturers on the market, Intel and AMD, launched several processor models with increasingly higher operating frequencies, they reached the physical limit of space in which the high temperatures generated by the processors could no longer be dissipated by conventional means, and this generated high temperatures in the other hardware components. So one solution that manufacturers came up with was to build processors that didn't need high operating frequency rates, but instead more balanced rates and a greater number of cores, i.e. multi-core processors (ALMEIDA, 2009).

The use of multiprocessors has significantly increased processing power, but energy consumption has remained a constant concern for engineers. With the advent of mobile devices, the concern about computer hardware using less energy has been maximised, given that mobile device hardware is fairly minimalist when compared to larger computers such as servers and clusters.

Dynamic Power Management (DPM) aims to reduce energy consumption at runtime. Different approaches have been proposed to selectively switch off/paralyse idle hardware components. For processors, manufacturers have developed various techniques for power management, allowing the processor to assume low-power states or to dynamically scale its voltage and frequency.

To regulate the low-power states, an Advanced Configuration and Power Interface (ACPI[1]) is used (ACPI, 2013). ACPI contains standards for the operating system to carry out configuration, power management and thermal management of devices. Technologies such as Turbo Boost 2.0 (INTEL, 2015), created by Intel and used in its processors, and AMD Cool'n Qui- et (AMD, 2004), created by AMD, are examples of this form of management.

Based on the unique ACPI interfaces of each processor, manufacturers have developed methods for processor-independent dynamic scaling of voltage and frequency (EDTF), making it possible to adjust the operating frequency of the CPUs at user level, reducing the current/voltage of the processors and, consequently, energy consumption. The CPUFreq used in the Linux Kernel is an example of this form of management (ALMEIDA, 2009).

Given the issues raised about the energy consumed by the CPU(s) when processing information, this work aims to study the dynamic scaling of processor voltage and frequency using CPUFreq, presenting its operation in different usage scenarios, and demonstrating the implementation of a new CPUFreq regulator for managing the energy consumed by the CPU(s).

The content of this work is divided into 6 chapters, as detailed below:

---

[1] ACPI is an industrial specification for realising power management and thermal management of mobile devices, desktops and servers via the operating system.

Chapter 1 - The introduction presents the context and motivation for the work.

Chapter 2 - In this chapter, we present the main objective of this work, which is to build a new regulator for managing the energy spent by the CPU(s), and the steps that will be taken to do so.

Chapter 3 - In this chapter, we highlight the concern about managing the energy consumption of processors, as well as the solutions developed by the main processor manufacturers and the solution created by the free software community.

Chapter 4 - This chapter shows the materials used to build the proposed regulator. The settings made in the operating system, the formulae used in the calculations, the configuration of the computer used in this work, the files contained in the /proc and /sys directories of the Kernel that were accessed to collect the necessary data, and the explanation of the algorithm for the proposed regulator.

Chapter 5 - This chapter shows, through graphs and discussions, what results were obtained by running the new regulator compared to the Ondemand regulator, the efficiency achieved by each of them, the influence of the sampling rate adopted, the influence of the operating frequency value of the CPU(s), and in what aspects the proposed regulator achieved improvements in the energy management of the processor.

Chapter 6 - This chapter shows the results of the studies and the construction of the new regulator for energy management in the CPU(s), how this new regulator met the expectations of the problem raised in the motivation for the work, as well as the theoretical contribution to new research on the subject, discussing and reflecting on what has already been done and providing a basis for new decision-making.

CHAPTER 2

OBJECTIVES

In this chapter, we present the objectives of this work and the steps that will be taken to achieve them.

2.1 GENERAL OBJECTIVE

Develop a CPUFreq regulator to manage the energy expended by the CPU(s).

2.2 SPECIFIC OBJECTIVES

- Carry out a literature review on the CPUFreq subsystem;
- Collect the data generated from the configuration files in the CPUFreq kernel module, organise them in graphs and analyse them so that the new regulator proposed in this work can be built;
- Build a new regulator for power management of the CPU(s), based on the utilisation rate of the processor;
- Create test environments with light, moderate and intense workloads to measure the efficiency of processor power management with the CPUFreq Userspace regulator, at static frequencies to evaluate processor utilisation;
- Run the new controller in test environments. Environments designed to evaluate processor utilisation and how the new controller will make frequency change decisions to possibly save energy spent by the CPU(s).

CHAPTER 3

THEORETICAL BACKGROUND

In this chapter, we highlight the concern about managing energy consumption by processors, as well as the solutions developed by the main processor manufacturers and the solution created by the free software community.

From 1996 onwards, desktop computers began to use a power monitoring and device configuration interface specification, the Advanced Configuration and Power Interface - ACPI, a technology co-developed by the manufacturers: Hewlett-Packard, Intel, Microsoft, Phoenix and Toshiba. ACPI allows power monitoring to be configured via the operating system, which enables more advanced configuration. The objectives of ACPI are: to facilitate and implement power monitoring functions; to improve power monitoring and its robustness; and to create a robust interface for device configuration.

With the availability of ACPI, other technologies and drivers were developed by computer manufacturers and the community, such as CPUFreq, which is the Linux Kernel module or subsystem responsible for managing the power expended by the CPU(s), implemented from Kernel 2.6 onwards; Intel Turbo Boost, which is the technology used by Intel in its processors to manage the processing efficiency and power of the CPU(s); and AMD cool'n Quiet, already mentioned above.

3.1 PROCESSOR MANAGEMENT TECHNOLOGIES

The power consumption of microprocessors depends directly on the core voltage and the operating frequency. The core voltage, in turn, also depends directly on the operating frequency, so for the microprocessor to operate at a low voltage, it is also necessary to reduce its frequency. Based on this relationship between operating frequency, core voltage and energy consumption, most of today's processors have mechanisms for saving energy by changing frequency and voltage at runtime. Frequency and voltage shifting techniques are known as dynamic frequency and voltage scaling, respectively, and were initially applied to mobile devices to extend battery life without compromising performance (VIEIRA NETO, 2011).

ACPI technology has allowed efficient initiatives to be developed and, in this work, we will focus more on CPUFreq because it is an open source technology, which has allowed access to design and implementation information, as well as its configuration files in the Kemel Linux module. The other two technologies mentioned, Turbo Boost Intel 2.0 and AMD Cool'n Quiet, are from proprietary companies, which made it impossible to access in-depth design and implementation information.

3.1.1CPUFreq of the Linux Kernel

One of the existing technologies that deals with managing the energy spent by the processor is CPUFreq. CPUFreq is a subsystem or module of Kemel Linux which, based on the scaling mechanisms mentioned above, makes it possible to improve the system's energy efficiency by regulating the processor's frequency and voltage at runtime. This subsystem is made up of three types of elements - frequency regulators (green), a core (yellow) and device drivers (blue) - which are detailed in the figure below:

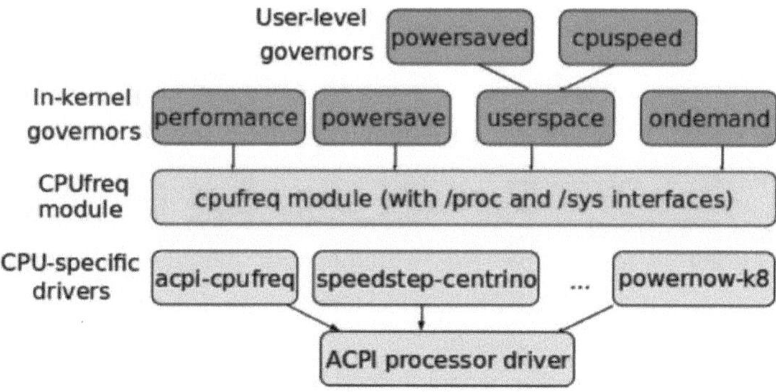

Figura 1 - Elements of the CPUFreq subsystem

Source: PALLIPADI, V.; STARIKOVSKIY, A. (2006, p. 223-238)

Frequency controllers are algorithms loaded into the CPUFreq subsystem or kernel module, responsible for implementing different processor frequency control policies. The following figure shows the main CPUFreq controllers:

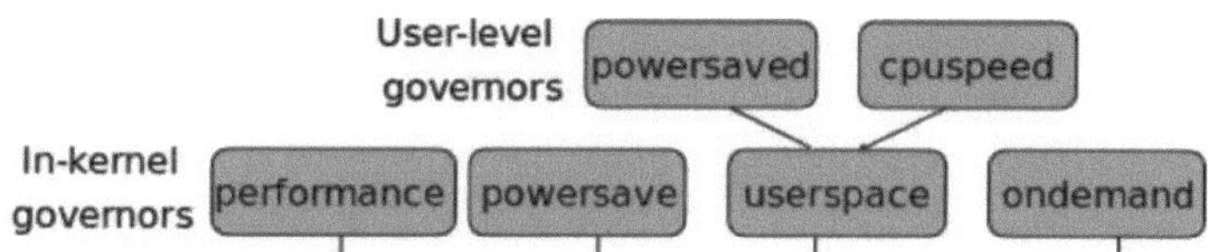

Figura 2 - CPUFreq frequency regulators
Source: Adapted by the author from PALLIPADI, V.; STARIKOVSKIY, A. (2006, p. 223-238)

In general, these regulators can be categorised into two types: static and dynamic. Static regulators only define a general frequency control policy, favouring, for example, performance or energy saving. The *"Performance", "Powersave"* and *"Userspace" controllers,* which respectively keep the processor at the highest and lowest available frequency, and at a user-defined minimum *(powersaved)* or maximum *(cpuspeed)* value, are examples of static controllers built into CPUFreq.

Dynamic regulators, on the other hand, base their frequency control policy on the periodic evaluation of some indicator - typically processor utilisation - determining, after each evaluation, the appropriate operating frequency. An example of a dynamic regulator built into CPUFreq is *"Ondemand",* which, in order to balance performance and energy efficiency, increases the processor's operating frequency when its utilisation rate is high and decreases it to save energy when a light load is observed

(PALLIPADI, 2006).

Only one frequency regulator can be active in the system at any given time. One regulator is set during system initialisation, but another regulator can be selected at runtime.

The CPUFreq kernel is responsible for mediating communication between regulators and drivers via the /proc and /sys subsystems. Both regulators and drivers must register with the kernel and offer a predefined set of interfaces in these subsystems. Through these interfaces, a regulator can, for example, ask the driver to inform it of the available operating frequencies or to make the microprocessor operate at a certain frequency. The CPUFreq core also implements, via sysfs[2] , an interface that allows the selection of the active frequency regulator to be changed at runtime. The following figure illustrates the structure of the core:

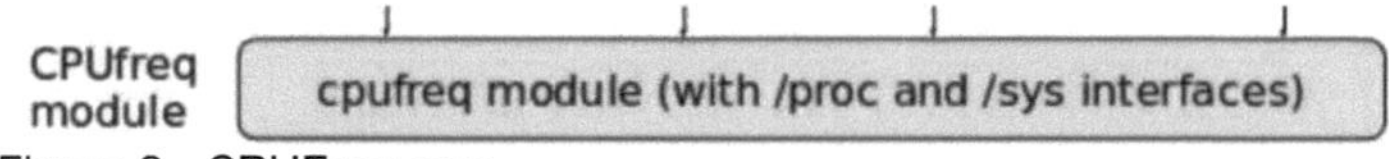

Figure 3 - CPUFreq core

Source: Adapted by the author from PALLIPADI, V.; STARIKOVSKIY, A. (2006, p. 223-238)

Device drivers implement the low-level mechanisms needed to control the frequency and voltage of the CPU(s). These mechanisms are platform-specific. Each different technology needs a specific driver. As the core voltage is dependent on the operating frequency, the core voltage is controlled by the driver according to the frequency change.

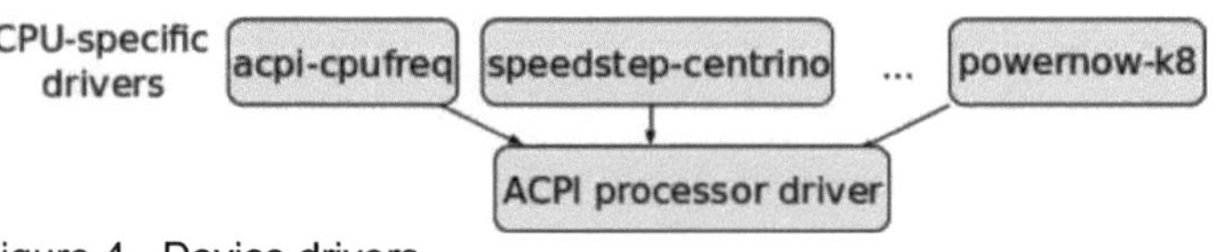

Figure 4 - Device drivers

[2] Sysfs is a file system that provides a means of exporting Kemel's data structures, their attributes and the links between them to the user's environment (MOCHEL; MURPHY, 2011).

Source: Adapted by the author from PALLIPADI, V.; STARIKOVSKIY, A. (2006, p. 223-238)

In addition to the policies implemented by its built-in controllers, CPUFreq can dynamically incorporate other frequency control options by installing new controllers implemented as Kernel modules. CPUFreq also allows the incorporation of controllers executed in user space by providing a special inbuilt controller *(Userspacé)* and a set of interfaces via sysfs. Regulators run in user space have the advantage of being easier to implement than regulators built into Kemel, however, they require context switching at each run, which results in a greater expenditure of resources. The regulators built into Kemel, on the other hand, can benefit from the Kernel's own interfaces and internal data structures, as well as not suffering from the resource costs associated with context switches.

3.1.1 CPUFreq regulators

As previously mentioned, a governor is an algorithm with pre-configured frequency settings for the CPU. These governors have to be loaded as Kernel modules to be accessed by other programmes on the system. It is possible to load several regulators as Kernel modules, however, there cannot be more than one regulator handling the CPU frequency. The regulators currently available are: (I) Performance: sets the CPU(s) to the maximum frequency; (II) Ondemand: Dynamically increases or decreases the frequency of the CPU(s) based on the needs of the system; (III) Conservative: similar to *"Ondemand"*, but more conservative, it sets the frequency of the CPU(s) non-suddenly and is based on utilisation averages to gradually change the frequency; (IV) Powersave: opposite to the *"Performance"* regulator, as it sets the CPU(s) to the minimum frequency; (V) Userspace: this regulator makes it possible to set the CPU(s) operating frequency to a static value defined by the user.

3.1.2 Conservative Regulator

Conservative is a regulator that changes the CPU frequency gradually and not directly to its upper limit value. If there is constant CPU activity, this regulator will increase the frequency in small jumps, for example from 1.0 GHz to 1.1GHz, 1.2GHz, 1.3 GHz and so on. In this way, energy savings with this regulator in operation are more efficient than with Ondemand (BRODOWSKI, 2014).

3.1.4 Ondemand regulator

Ondemand is a regulator that comes by default in the Linux Kernel, from version 2.6.9 onwards (PALLIPADI; STARIKOVSKIY, 2006). It changes the CPU frequency to the maximum limit when CPU activity is high, on average greater than or equal to 95%, and gradually decreases when this activity is minimised. This is a regulator that has a certain efficiency because it only increases the CPU frequency when its utilisation is high; however, it does not provide satisfactory energy savings because it quickly sets the frequency to its maximum value, thus using more energy (PALLIPADI, 2006; BRODOWSKI, 2014).

3.1.5 Powersave regulator

The Powersave is a regulator that adjusts the frequency of the CPU(s) to the lowest value within the range between the maximum frequency and the minimum frequency. It is the regulator with the greatest energy saving gains, since it only works at the lowest operating frequency of the CPU(s). However, this comes at a cost, the loss of efficiency of the processor, since it will not be able to work at frequencies higher than the lowest possible for the CPU(s) (BRODOWSKI, 2014).

3.1.6 Performance regulator

Performance is a regulator that adjusts the operating frequency of the CPU(s) to the highest value within the range between the maximum frequency and the minimum frequency. In this way, there is a greater gain in efficiency for the CPU(s), but there are no energy savings due to the CPU(s) working at the highest possible frequency for that architecture (BRODOWSKI, 2014).

3.1.7 Userspace regulator

This controller belongs to the category of static controllers found in the Linux Kernel, as it is only possible to configure a single operating frequency value for the CPU(s).

Userspace is a regulator that makes it possible to adjust the operating frequency of the CPU(s) to a static value, according to the values available for the CPU. If the change is made via the command line, the user must have root privileges[3] to do so, and if the change is made via the graphical interface, the cpufreq-indicator application[4] can be used. The following figure shows the indicator:

---

[3] On GNU/Linux systems, the root user has all possible privileges for administering the operating system.

[4] cpufreq-indicator is a desktop application for the GNU/Linux system that is used to intuitively choose the regulator that will operate in the processor's power management, as well as choosing static frequencies for the CPU(s) operation.

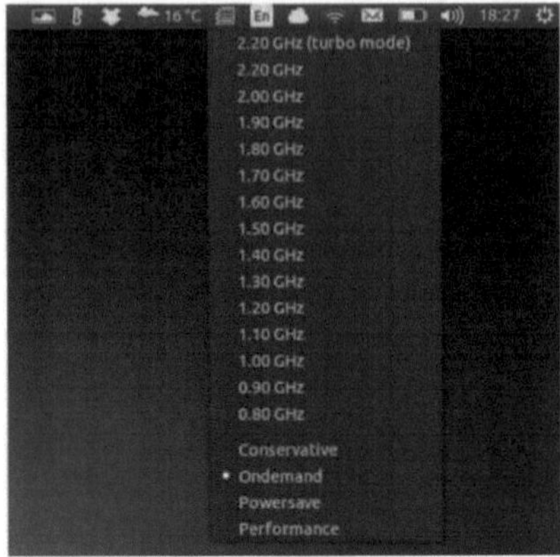

Figure 5 - indicator-cpufreq application for changing frequency

Source: http://inversotech.com.br/wp-content/uploads/2014/01/indicator-cpufreq.png

3.1.8 Intel Turbo Boost 2.0

Turbo Boost is a technology implemented by Intel in certain versions of its CPU(s) that automatically allows the processor cores to work faster than they would at the standard operating frequency when they are operating below the specified limits for power, current and temperature. When the processor is not at its thermal and electrical limit and the running workload demands it, the voltage and frequency of the cores can be increased according to the microarchitecture implemented in them. If it's Nehalem, the increase will be 133MHz at a time, if it's based on Sandy Bridge technology, the increase will be 100MHz at a time. The technology is activated when the operating system requests a frequency higher than the processor's default or the current frequency at which it is operating, as long as this is not higher than the upper limit frequency. (INTEL, 2014).

The maximum Turbo Boost 2.0 frequency is the highest achieved by the processor when conditions permit, depending on the workload, hardware, software and system settings. The availability and frequency utilisation of the Turbo Boost 2.0

technology state depends on various factors such as: (I) Type of workload; (II) Number of active cores; (III) Estimated current consumption; (IV) Estimated power consumption; (V) Processor temperature.

When the processor is operating below these limits and the user's workload requires additional performance, the processor frequency will increase dynamically until the upper frequency limit is reached (INTEL, 2014).

3.1.9 AMD Cool'n Quiet

AMD Cool'n Quiet is a technology developed by AMD that makes it possible to change the operating frequency of the computer's CPU(s) while it is running. Similar to the CPUFreq and Intel Turbo Boost 2.0 technologies, AMD Cool'n Quiet also decreases or increases the processor's frequency rate, taking into account the idle time the computer can be found in at any given moment. If the computer is idle enough, AMD Cool'n Quiet lowers the frequency of the CPU(s) to save energy and also lowers the fan speed to minimise fan noise. When the utilisation rate of the processor increases, AMD Cool'n Quiet increases the operating frequency of the CPU(s), and consequently the speed of the processor's fan (AMD, 2015).

CHAPTER 4

MATERIAL AND METHODS

This chapter shows the materials used to build the proposed regulator. The settings made in the operating system, the formulae used in the calculations, the settings of the computer used in this work, and how the Kernel files contained in the /proc and /sys directories were accessed to collect the necessary data, as well as an explanation of the proposed regulator algorithm.

4.1 MATERIAL

The need for a computer that was always available to carry out the experiments, as well as to make changes to the regulator algorithm and constantly analyse the results, motivated the use of a personal notebook rather than a laboratory machine. Thus, the experiments in this work were carried out on a Dell notebook with the following configurations:

- Vostro 5470 A50 model;
- Intel® Core™ Í7-4500U CPU @ 1.80GHz x 4;
- 8Gb of RAM;
- 500Gb 5400 rpm Sata hard drive;
- NVIDIA GeForce GT 740M 2Gb video card;
- the operating system used was GNU/Linux Ubuntu in version 12.04 LTS, as its Kernel allowed access to the Userspace regulator and frequency changes in userspace. In the current version of GNU/Linux Ubuntu 14.04 LTS, this type of configuration was not possible;
- the cpufreq-utils application, version 0.07, as this is the version available

on GNU/Linux Ubuntu 12.04 LTS.

The software applications used to generate the light, moderate and heavy workloads were, respectively:

- the song on000001.mp3[5] , played in Ubuntu's default music player, Rhythmbox[6] ;

-the Citizen Engineering video[7] , volume 1, phones, running on Ubuntu's default video player, Totem[8] ;

-and the hard disc performance measurement application Bonnie++[9] .

4.2 METHODS

After studying the Kemel Linux CPUFreq documentation, statistical data was collected from the file */proc/stat*[10] , where there are counters, and the number of counters depends on the Kernel version, with 10 being the number in the version used in this work, which is Kernel 3.13, each responsible for storing values related to various pieces of information used by Kemel. The first lines of this file, obtained with the *cat/proc/stat* command, are shown in the table below:

Table 1 - Statistical data extracted from the /proc/stat file

Name	user	nice	System	idle	iowait	irq	softirq	steal	guest	guest_nice
cpu	471562	4225	121050	7479385	49974	3	179	0	0	0
cpuO	123850	2123	37101	2416561	40973	2	133	0	0	0

[5] Available at <http://www.dominiopublico.gov.br/download/som/on000001.mp3>
[6] Available at <http://projects.gnome.org/rhythrnbox/>
[7] Available at <https://www.youtube.com/watch7v-ikOgzOApIc>
[8] Available at <http://www.gnome.org/projects/totem/>
[9] Available at <http://sourceforge.net/projects/bonnie/>
[10] /proc/stat contains data related to processor utilisation. This file is read by the power manager, and the frequency chosen for the processor to operate at is written to the CPUFreq interface.

cpul	119394	1059	24714	1689428	2464	0	11	0	0	0
cpu2	118133	695	30416	1683314	4479	0	27	0	0	0
cpu3	110184	348	28817	1690081	2057	0	7	0	0	0

Source: Prepared by the author

As shown in the table above, the last four rows represent the values of each CPU in the computer. The second row, called cpu, represents the sum of the counter values for each CPU plus 1. Each column corresponds to a counter that is incremented when a certain activity is carried out on the processor:

- user: corresponds to the number of processes running in user space;
- nice: corresponds to the number of processes running in user space and with low priority;

-system : corresponds to the number of processes running in core space;

-idle : corresponds to the value incremented when the processor is idle;

-iowait : corresponds to the number of input/output operations waiting to be completed;

-irq : is the number of interruption services;

-softirq : corresponds to the number of software interrupt services;

-steal : this is the time used to run other operating systems in a virtualised environment;

-guest : time spent running a virtual cpu for another operating system under the control of the Linux operating system kernel;

-guest_nice : corresponds to the execution of a remote virtual guest process.

The counters' statistical data was collected using the command *file = fopen("/proc/stat", "r"),* which opens the file to read the data, and *fscanf(file,"%d", &<parameter name>),* which reads the data and stores it in the variable corresponding to the *parameter.*

In order to measure the ratio of the processor's idle time to the sampling period, it was necessary to take into account that the counters in the /proc/stat file are always incremented. The counters in /proc/stat were incremented by calculating the ratio between the difference between the current and previous values in the *idle* column *Idle(t) - Idle(t -1)* and the difference between the current and previous sum of the counters in the cpu line Counterft) - *Counter(t -1),* at a time instant *t* (LUIZ, 2012), according to the following formula:

$$increment\,(t) = \frac{\Delta\ Idle}{\Delta\ Counter} \qquad (1)$$

To calculate processor utilisation, the formula below was used, where utilisation was defined as 0 complement of *increment(t)* illustrated in the formula above:

$$utilisation(t) = 1\text{-}increment\ (t) \quad (2)$$

For the sampling time used in our regulator, we consider the sampling policy used in the Ondemand regulator. In the Ondemand regulator, the sampling time is equal to 1000 * 10ps, the latter parameter being the transition latency, i.e. the time interval that the Kernel checks for changes in the processes' utilisation of the processor. These values are stored in the counters shown in table 1.

In the proposed regulator, we adopted the value of 10000 times the transition latency, considering that the statistical data obtained with this sampling value was more satisfactory, given that if a small sampling period is adopted, the output value calculated by formula (1) above will be small. However, if the sampling period is too long, high processor utilisation may occur in a short interval within the sampling time, but it may not be possible for the regulator to take action in the face of this rapid change in workload, a perspective that corroborates the thinking of Saulo (2012, p. 115), who applied a similar sampling policy in his doctoral work on power management in processors with time-varying workloads through a microcontroller, stating that

> [...] it is not interesting to adopt a very small sampling period, because the resolution of the output will be small. Nor is it interesting to adopt too large a sampling period, because high utilisation due to a burst load during a short time interval during the sampling period can be filtered out, and there will be no reaction in the controller to this change in workload.

To run the workloads, it was necessary to disable three of the four processor cores used, so that there would be no processing parallelism when running the workloads, and with processing on just one core, the results would be satisfactory.

The three cores were deactivated via a configuration file in the Linux command terminal, by accessing the */sys/devices/system/cpu/ directory,* where there are directories for each processor core along with their configuration files. The command to deactivate a core is *echo 0 > Online, with* the *online* parameter being the variable that stores two possible values: 1 for an active core and 0 for an inactive one.

The workloads were divided into three types: light load, moderate load and heavy load. They were executed constantly, contrary to Saulo's (2012) idea of executing workloads in bursts, because in our work we prioritised executing the new regulator in an environment with a constant demand for processing requests. All the workloads were executed during the 1000 iterations of the proposed regulator.

In the light load only the public domain song on000001.mp3 was played in the Rhythmbox music player, version 2.96. The moderate load ran the public domain video citizenengine-ervm.mov, in the Totem video player, version 3.0.1. Finally, the heavy workload ran the hard disc performance measurement application, Bonnie++.

The steps carried out by the proposed regulator were: (I) reading the counter values from the */proc/stat* file and calculating the quantisation using formula (1); (II) calculating the utilisation using formula (2), according to the criterion adopted by the condition that if the utilisation of the processor *utilisation(t)* is equal to 1, i.e. 100%, new requests will not be served immediately, so a penalty value will be calculated *penalty(t),* as illustrated in the following formula:

$$penalidade(t) = \begin{cases} 1, \text{ se } utilização(t) = 1 \\ 0, \text{ caso contrário} \end{cases} \quad (3)$$

(III) if *utilisation(t)* is equal to 1, increase the operating frequency of the CPU(s) by 0.1GHz, otherwise decrease the operating frequency of the CPU(s) by 0.1GHz.

Therefore, in order to manage the energy spent by the CPU(s), the regulator we propose takes into account the utilisation rate to configure the CPU(s) operating frequency at runtime, seeking the minimum value whenever possible.

Naturally, at times of high processing demand, a frequency rate will be chosen that is sufficient to avoid a penalty. This implies making more power available to the processor at the expense of greater energy expenditure.

The flowchart below illustrates how our regulator's algorithm works and when the decision is made based on the utilisation rate.

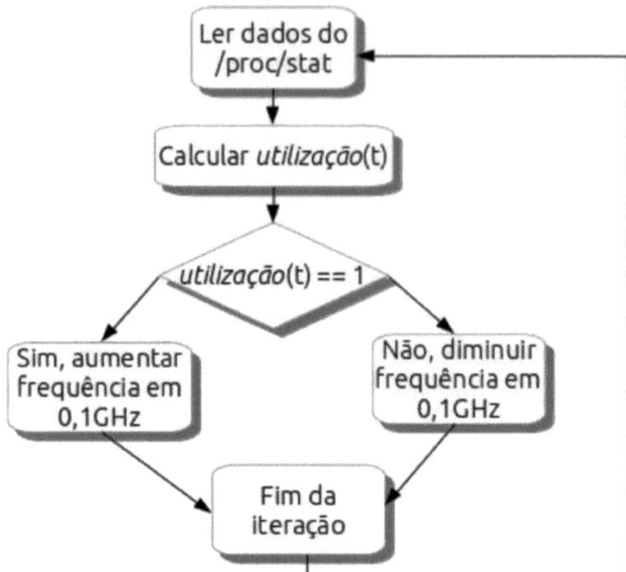

Figure 6 - Flowchart of the proposed regulator

Source: Prepared by the author

CHAPTER 5

RESULTS AND DISCUSSIONS

This chapter shows, with graphs and discussions, what results were obtained by running the new regulator compared to the Ondemand regulator, the efficiency achieved by each of them, the influence of the sampling rate adopted, the influence of the operating frequency value of the CPU(s), and in what respects the proposed regulator achieved improvements in the energy management of the processor.

The sampling rate considerably affects how a controller filters out variations in the utilisation rate of the CPU(s). The values tested in this work were: 0.ls; 0.2s; 0.3s; 0.4s and 0.5s. For the value of 0.ls, a more accurate variation in processor utilisation was detected during the execution of the moderate workload.

The efficiency obtained in the previous result with a sampling rate of 0.ls is not repeated when we use higher values, for the reasons discussed above, i.e. that if a small sampling period is adopted, the calculated output value will be small, however, if the sampling period is too long, a high utilisation of the processor may occur in a short interval within the sampling time, but it will not be filtered and it will not be possible for the regulator to take action in the face of this rapid change in workload, as can be seen in graph 1 below:

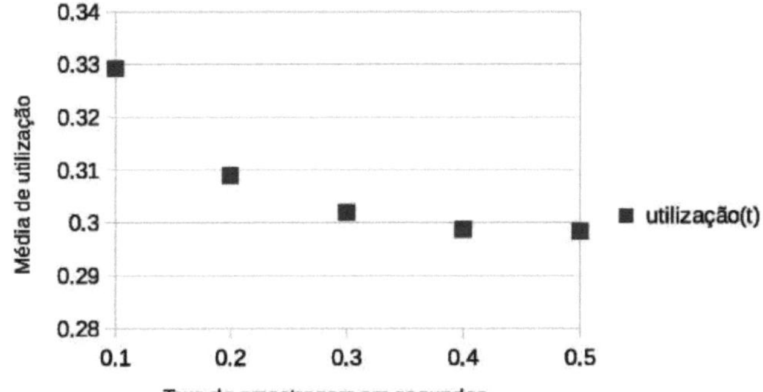

Graph 1 - Utilisation X number of iterations for the 1.3GHz frequency and variable sampling rate

Source: Prepared by the author

The comparison between the values for the sampling rate, and the choice of 0.ls, reinforces what was mentioned earlier about the time interval for sampling, as it is not feasible to adopt an interval that is too large or too small in order to obtain more efficient filtering.

The value of the operating frequency must always be changed to meet the processing demands of the operating system. When the frequency value is high, the running process will finish as soon as possible, however, after it finishes, the processor will remain idle for some time, operating at a high frequency until the execution of another process is requested by the operating system. Thus, it is true that a dynamic frequency change is applied to efficiently save energy spent by the CPU. To more clearly represent the influence of the operating frequency value, let's look at graph 2 below:

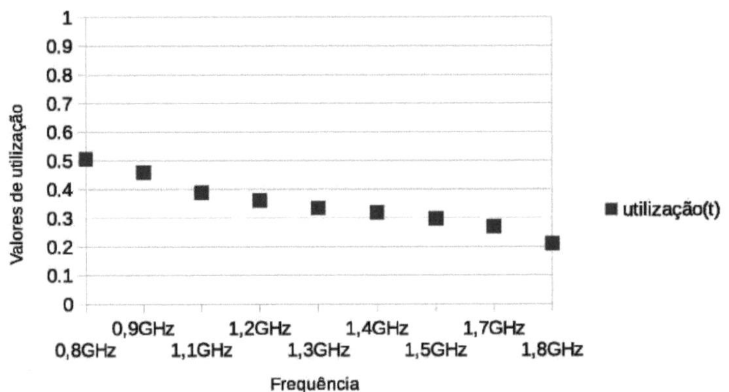

Graph 2 - Utilisation X variant frequency and 0.ls sampling rate

Source: Prepared by the author

5.1 NEW REGULATOR

The proposed regulator takes into account the value of the processor utilisation rate to dynamically configure the value of the CPU(s) operating frequency, seeking the minimum frequency whenever possible. The decision is made by checking the current utilisation of the processor. If there is 100 per cent processing demand, the operating frequency value will be increased by 0.1GHz each iteration until it reaches the processor's maximum operating frequency value, and if demand is not 100 per cent, it will be decreased by 0.1GHz each iteration until it reaches the processor's minimum operating frequency value. The following figure illustrates the part of the code where our regulator makes its decision:

```
if(ys_t >= 1 && valor_frequencia < 1800000){
        valor_frequencia = (valor_frequencia + 100000);
        sprintf(comando, "cpufreq-set -f %d", valor_frequencia);
        system(comando);
}
else if(ys_t < 1 && valor_frequencia > 768000){
        valor_frequencia = (valor_frequencia - 100000);
        sprintf(comando, "cpufreq-set -f %d", valor_frequencia);
        system(comando);
}
```

Figure 7 - Decision structure of the new regulator
Source: Prepared by the author

In the proposed regulator, the frequency is only changed to the maximum rate if a 100 per cent processing demand occurs, as it makes no sense to keep the CPU(s) wasting energy while there is constant processor idleness, or a light workload is being carried out.

The Ondemand regulator configures the processor's operating frequency policy a little differently. If there is more than 95% utilisation, it already changes the frequency value to the maximum supported by the CPU(s), and this is not done gradually. It is the decrease in frequency that is done gradually.

In a time-varying workload, starting with a heavy load, followed by a light load, and ending with a moderate load, the latter two being interspersed with the heavy load, we can see that the utilisation rate varies a lot when the processing also fluctuates, and this doesn't happen in the heavy load, because the processor is under a very high processing demand. Analysing how the new regulator and the Ondemand regulator filtered processor utilisation in the scenario described above, we can see that the new regulator filtered the variations in CPU(s) utilisation more efficiently. As can be seen in graphs 3 and 4 below:

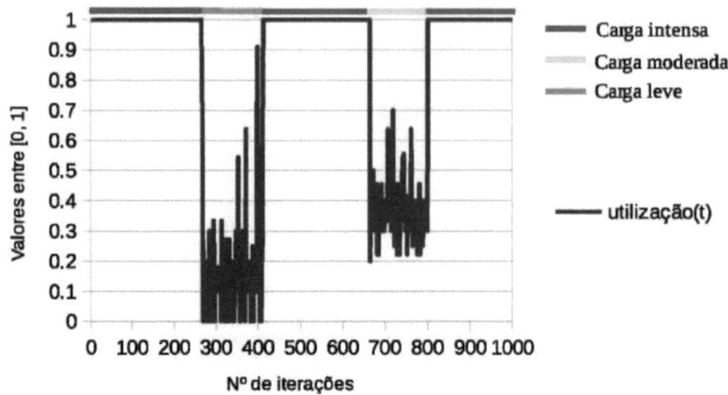

Graph 3 - Calculation of processor utilisation carried out by the new controller under a time-varying load and a sampling rate of 0.ls

Source: Prepared by the author

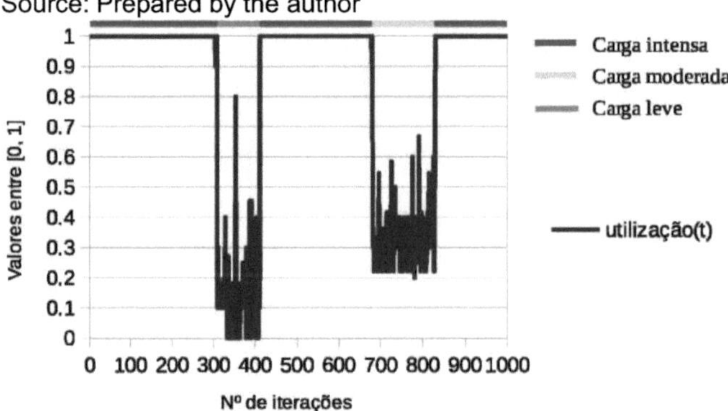

Graph 4 - Calculation of processor utilisation carried out by the Ondemand controller under a time-varying load and a sampling rate of 0.ls

Source: Prepared by the author

With high processor utilisation resulting from a heavy load, a penalty will occur at times. Therefore, new demands made by the operating system will not be served immediately, indicating that 100 per cent of the CPU(s) has been required. Our regulator's power management policy causes the frequency rate to gradually return to the lowest possible value in 0.1GHz intervals. However, to reach this minimum frequency, the Ondemand regulator spends more time. The behaviour described is exemplified in graphs 5 and 6 below:

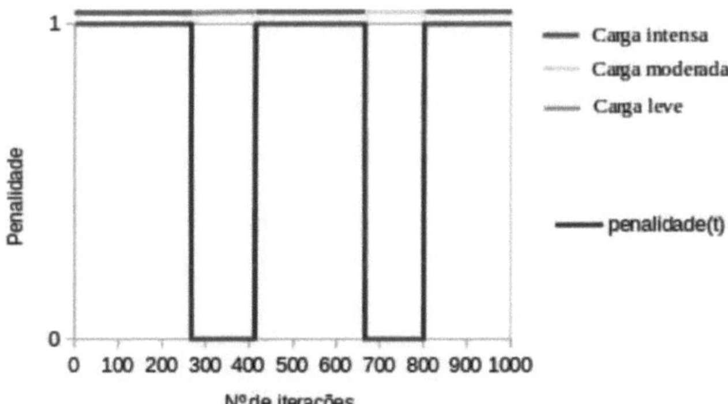

Graph 5 - Calculation of the processor penalty performed by the new regulator on a time-varying load and a sampling rate of 0.ls

Source: Prepared by the author

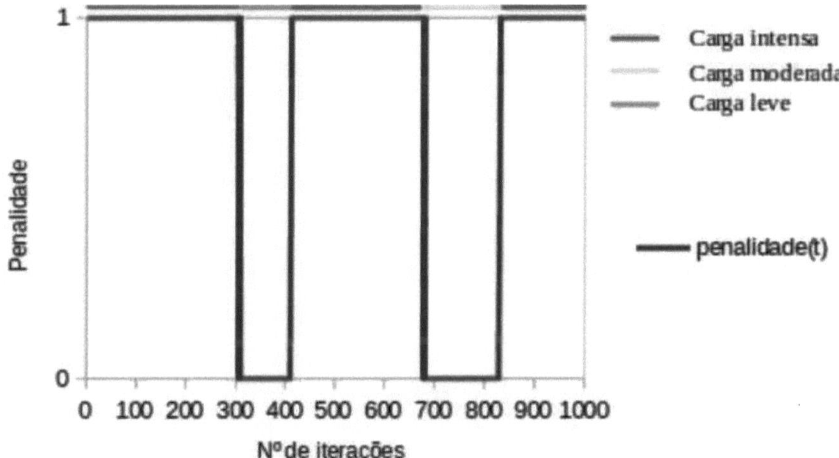

Graph 6 - Calculation of the processor penalty performed by the Ondemand controller under a time-varying load and a sampling rate of 0.ls

Source: Prepared by the author

When the operating system demanded maximum efficiency for processing the intense workload, the proposed regulator changed the operating frequency of the CPU(s) to the maximum value, 1.8GHz, and over time this value was reduced when the light workload started running, no longer demanding maximum efficiency from the processor.

For the light workload, our regulator maintained the minimum frequency value most of the time, and again, there was only a change in frequency when the heavy workload was again requested by the operating system and started running, causing our regulator to gradually change the frequency to the maximum value in a few moments.

Then the moderate load was carried out and the frequency was reduced again, and it rose again when the intense load was carried out again, ending the iterations.

The changes to the operating frequency of the CPU(s) made by the new regulator can be seen in Graph 7 below:

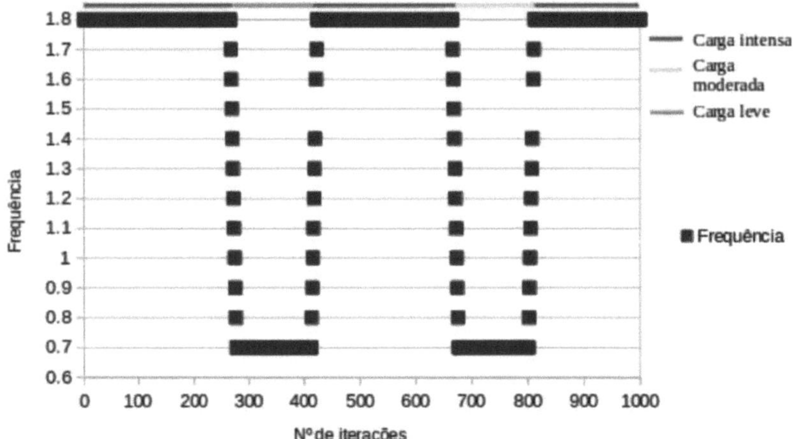

Graph 7 - Frequency X number of iterations with 0.ls sampling rate and time-varying workload

Source: Prepared by the author

The sampling rate, the utilisation calculation and the penalty calculation were the three indicators that made it feasible to process the information collected and used to run our regulator, and consequently to make satisfactory energy management decisions, when compared in the same respects with the Ondemand regulator, which took longer to reduce the processor frequency and therefore used more energy.

For high processing demands, both our regulator and Ondemand obtained similar results, however, when reducing the processor frequency, our regulator obtained a better result, culminating in a more efficient saving of the energy spent by the CPU(s).

CHAPTER 6

FINAL CONSIDERATIONS

The general purpose of this work was to build a new regulator for managing the energy spent by the CPU(s). Its comparison with the Ondemand regulator, which is the standard regulator in the current versions of the Linux Kernel, brought good learnings and showed that we were able to fulfil our proposal to build a new regulator for CPU(s) energy management.

The studies carried out were based on processor management technologies, namely: CPUFreq of the Linux kernel; CPUFreq regulators - Conservative, Ondemand, Userspace, Powersave and Performance, including, Intel Turbo Boost 2.0 and AMD Coll'n Quiet, in a less in-depth manner, due to the fact that these are proprietary technologies, which implies that it is not possible to have access to the documentation, design and implementation of the technologies.

As a result of the drafting of the new regulator, it was realised that existing solutions do not meet all the demands in this field, and there is a lot of research to be done on how to develop better techniques for the energy management of processors.

Dynamic regulators are those that best adapt to variations in workloads over time, so the construction of our regulator to dynamically manage the change in operating frequency of the CPU(s) for the best energy management of the CPU(s) met our initial expectations of contributing a new solution for managing energy expenditure in processors.

The use of a static regulator to manage processor energy consumption is unfeasible when dealing with time-varying workloads, because initially you don't know what type of workload the processor will be handling, so keeping it operating at just one frequency all the time will at some point result in a lack of performance or unnecessary energy consumption.

That said, using a dynamic regulator for energy management of processors is the most appropriate solution, given that information processing today is also dynamic and highly variable. Thus, we realised that the new regulator proposed in this study was able to adapt satisfactorily to the variations that occur in the processing of time-varying workloads, given that its execution was at user level and this implies that data needs to be read from files in the /proc and /sys directories, unlike the Ondemand regulator which is at Kernel level and thus has access to data directly in the Kernel without needing to read from files within directories.

The research has shed important light on how companies, represented by Intel and AMD, and the Linux community, represented by the open CPUFreq technology, have made efforts to minimise the energy consumption of existing computers and devices. It also confirms the feasibility of building a new regulator for processor power management and that there is still room for improvement in the current proposals. In addition, it is hoped that this work can contribute to the emergence of a new solution for managing the energy used by current processors, at the level of the Linux operating system kernel. It is also hoped that it will be a study that can contribute theoretically to further research on the subject.

CHAPTER 7

REFERENCES

ACPI. Advanced Configuration & Power Interface. Available at: <http://www.acpi.info/>. Accessed on: 27 Nov. 2015.

ALMEIDA, Rafael Bruno. Evolution of Processors: Comparison of intel and AMD processor families, 2009. Available at: <http://www.ic.unicamp.br/~ducatte/mo401/ls2009/T2/089065-t2.pdf>. Accessed on: 11 October 2014.

AMD. CooTn Quiet™: Technology Installation Guide for AMD Athlon™ 64 Processor Based Systems. 2004. Available at: <http://web.archive.org/web/20070409045621/http://www.amd.com/us-en/assets/content_type/DownloadableAssets/Cool_N_Quiet_Installation_Guide3.pdf >. Accessed on: 28 January 2015.

BRODOWSKI, Dominik. LinuxCPUFreqiUSERGUIDE. 2014. Available at: <https://www.kernel.org/doc/Documentation/cpu-freq/user-guide.txt>. Accessed on: 06 October 2014.

.LinuxCPUFreq:CPUFreqGovernors - information for users and de- velopers. 2014. Available at: <https://www.kernel.org/doc/Documentation/cpu- freq/governors.txt>. Accessed on: 06 October 2014.

.LinuxCPUFreq:CPUDrivers. 2014. Available at: <https://www.kernel.org/doc/Documentation/cpu-freq/cpu-drivers.txt>. Accessed on: 06 October 2014.

INTEL. Intel Turbo Boost Technology 2.0: brave overview. 2014. Available at: <http://www.intel.com.br/content/www/br/pt/architecture-and-technology/turbo-boost/turbo- boost-technology.html>. Accessed on: 10 October 2014.

LUIZ, Saulo Oliveira Dornellas. **Dynamic Power Management in Processors with**

Time-varying Workloads. 2012.148 f. Thesis (PhD) - Postgraduate Programme in Electrical Engineering, Federal University of Campina Grande, Campina Grande, 2012.

MOCHEL, Patrick; MURPHY, Mike. Sysfs: The filesystem for exporting kernel objects. 2011. Available at: <https://www.kernel.org/doc/Documentation/filesystems/sysfs.txt>. Accessed on: 28 January 2015.

PALLIPADI, Venkatesh. Linuxcpufreq-statsdriver: Information for users. 2014. Available at: <https://www.kemel.org/doc/Documentation/cpu-freq/CPUFreq-stats.txt>. Accessed on: 06 October 2014.

PALLIPADI, V.; STARIKOVSKIY, A. The ondemand governor. In: **Proceedings of the Linux Symposium.** [S.L: s.n.], 2006. v. 2, p. 215-230. (document), 4.3.1, 4.3, 4.3.1, 4.3.1, 4.4.

VIEIRA NETO, Lourival. **Lunatik:** Operating System Kernel Scripting with Lua. 2011. 69 f. Dissertation (Master's Degree) - Postgraduate Programme in Informatics, Department of Informatics, Pontifical Catholic University of Rio de Janeiro, Rio de Janeiro, 2011. Chap. 4.

Printed by Books on Demand GmbH, Norderstedt / Germany